My Colorful Thoughts

Melissa Edwards

BookLeaf Publishing

Presentation by *BookLeaf Publishing*

Web: www.bookleafpub.com

E-mail: info@bookleafpub.com

ISBN: 9789357440622

First edition 2023

What Can A Line Do?

What can a line drawn with a black pen do?
It can provide an area to be filled with color.
What can the color being added do?
It can add life to a picture.
What can that picture do?
It can illustrate a positive message.
What can that positive message do?
It can inspire a glimmer of hope.
What can that glimmer do?
It can transform into a flowing stream of thoughts.
What can that flowing stream of thoughts do?
It can cause a smile.
What can that smile do?
It can reflect the JOY in your heart!

Actions of Color

Color is all around us

Color can shout
Color can whisper
Color can sing
Color can create
Color can brighten the day
Color can reflect your deepest darkest feelings
Color can be simple
Color can be complicated
Color can be vibrant
Color can be muted
Color can evoke a memory
Color can cause a wave of emotions
Color can weave back together a broken heart
Color can pull up the strength needed to face
what is up ahead

Color is also within us

What Can Your Paintbrush Do?

My paintbrush makes beautiful colors come alive
My paintbrush can also make a mess of colors
blended together
My paintbrush sings a beautiful song of harmony
My paintbrush can also fall off the edge
My paintbrush celebrates
My paintbrush can also make mistakes
My paintbrush listens and reacts
My paintbrush can also not follow directions
My paintbrush cheers me on my journey
My paintbrush can also let me know when it is
time to stop and wait
My paintbrush empowers me to tell a story
My paintbrush can also find ideas I never knew
existed

Get Started

I start with a plan in mind
Most of the time …
Should I pull out a canvas or paper?
Am I using watercolor or acrylic paint?
I really like that certain PINK …
Will it show up in this creation?
Or should I try to challenge myself to not use it?
But it makes me happy
So why not use it?
What should I start with?
The background?
The flowers in front?
I know I should start with the back and work forward
But that is not what I want to do'
And it is my creation
So it is my rules
Well not really rules
But inspiration
I may lose the idea and inspiration for the front if I start with the back
But I may get an even better idea starting at the back ..
If I keep asking questions, I may never get started …
So I am just going to start and see what happens …

Complicated and Simple

Paint the sky
I don't know if I can
It is blue
But it is just not that simple
It is blue
Look at the light
It is blue
Look at the darker area
It is blue
Look at the clouds

The sky is blue and the clouds are white
But it is not that simple
Some areas are transparent
While other areas are more opaque
Some areas come together
While others areas split apart
Some areas are circular
While others are waves

Paint the sky
Make it full if colors and shapes
Make it full of lights and darks
Make it full of hope and dreams
Make it complicated
But also make it simple

The Reason

Perfection is not my artistic goal anymore
Who wants straight lines and realistic representations
Embracing the movement of line art and color
In whimsical and wonky creations
My goal now is to share joy and love using my colorful creations
I work with the line that flows from inspiration to my black pen or paintbrush
If that line wiggles when it is supposed to be straight,
It used to stress me out and make me want to quit
But now I see that alteration as
Something to celebrate
A new opportunity to play
A chance to change my mind
A possibility that wasn't there before
If watercolor or acrylic paint flows out of the space outline for it,
That is an opportunity for the expression of more creativity.
Sharing joy and love inspired both by bible verses and inspirational quotes
Is the reason I let my black line flow and add bits of color

Options

Options can be a good thing
Look at all the possibilities
Think about all that potential
Options can be a scary thing
Look at the possibilities for mistakes
Think about all the potential struggles
Options can be a roadblock
That roadblock can stand in the way
But that roadblock could also force a new path
That new path will lead to more options
And possibly more roadblocks
But the key is to keep moving
Moving means making choices
And embracing options
All along the way

Listen to the Message

I started creating
I am drawing with a black pen
Because if I use a pencil
I erase too much
And never get to the fun part …
Adding the color
The color is what brings the drawings alive
Traditional colors are ok
But a bit boring at times
Where is that pop?
Where is the moment of joy?
Where is that surprise?
Should I start with yellow
Or purple
Or my favorite shade of pink
I must listen to the colors
Listen to the message
They want me to convey
The joy they want me to share

Color of Creativity?

What color is CREATIVITY?
I don't think it is just one color
Since creativity is not just one thing
There are so many aspects to creativity
Maybe each letter is a different color
Watercolors that blend into each others
But you have to be careful so it doesn't end up a mess
I think there is a line between messy and creative
Although it is a fine line and easily confused
It looks different to everybody
For me there is lots of purple
And bold, vibrant colors
But also a sense of calm to surprise you
Maybe add in some sparkles and glitter too ...

Where to Find It

Finding color in unexpected locations

Hearing children giggling

Discovering color combinations you wouldn't
think work together

Noticing details that spark ideas

Reading old books that have a story to tell
beyond just the one that is printed on the pages

Conversing with a friend

Enjoying musical notes and phrases that
encourage happiness and relaxation on the inside

Joy can show up in unanticipated places …

Potential

The color of happiness
It may vary for each person
But for me right now
It is a shade of pink
Not too light pink
Not too dark pink
Not too bright pink
But a joyous pink
That makes me smile
But really happiness is more
It is not just one color
Maybe a combination
Of individual colors
Maybe add yellow
Or purple
Or a fresh green
Not a mixture
Each color is independent
With its own unique qualities
But has even more power
When combined with another
Working together does not take away
But increases the potential

In and Out

Bubbles bumping into each other
Circles overlapping to share but divide
Wavy Lines filling in empty spaces
Small pieces joining together
Building up and out
But also forwards and backwards
Swooping up
Barrelling down
Twisting along the way
With words flying out and coming back in
That's what imagination looks like to me!

Notice

Inspiration comes
from the words I hear
and the images I see
in the world around me

I look and listen
for the joy and positivity
that many of us
do not notice
in our hectic lives

Listen to the Lines

Heavy watercolor paper
Serves as the foundation
For the black outlines
To begin each project

The resulting image
Lets me know to add color
And where
Whether to use
Acrylic paint
Watercolor paint
Or both

Adding color is like adding magic
To make the creation come alive

You Never Know

Embrace ideas
Arms open wide
Welcome inspiration
Discover motivation
Just start
Even if you don't really know
Just go
And let things flow
Look at it in a new way
Notice the sparks
Grab them
Those burning ideas
Don't let them get away
You may use them one day

How to do you paint hope?

To paint a picture of hope
Choose where to start
Do you begin at the side and move ahead?
Do you move to the back and start there?
Do you start with the present spark and leave the rest behind?
Choose a color to use
Yellow brings brightness
Blue can be calming
Maybe it is a combination
Green …
Purple …
A yellow circle in the middle
Should it go from bright to soft
Or soothing to impactful
Then blending to a soft orange
As the ideas involved get more solid
Let's go from a soft orange to the pink in a sunset
Hope is growing from the inside out

When You Are Stuck ...

Create Ideas
Bring the pieces together
Shake Ideas
Move them all around
Pour Ideas
Change the location
Sprinkle Ideas
Split and divide
Dance Ideas
Move to the music
Explore Ideas
Look for possibilities
Grow Ideas
From the bottom up or to the side
Smash Ideas
Break apart and put back together
Tackle Ideas
Lock in one location
Spread Ideas
Smooth and connect
Saute Ideas
Add in some spice
Embellish Ideas
Throw in the sparkle
Embrace Ideas
Wrap it up tight

Raindrops

What would it be like
If it rained all the time
Would all colors be more muted
I picture blues and greens
Fading into and out of each other
Adding water to the color
Would make it less vibrant
But would it be murky
Or would there be defined colors
Just darker ones
Maybe we could add some color
Since umbrellas and rain boots
Would be constant additions to wardrobes
Small pops of pink, yellow, and orange
To provide pops of brightness
And joy!

Collaboration of Color

It is a combination
But more like a collaboration
There are still unique qualities present
Of the two colors that joined together
And the tone of the result depends
On how much of each original color
Is present
A collaboration is when ideas come together
But still hold true in many ways
Purple

Drawing Flowers

Drawing flowers
Flowers that I see in my mind
Might look like actual flowers
But probably not
And that is ok
Drawing a shape in the middle
Not quite a circle
But a shape with rounded edges
Maybe a rounded triangle shape
For a petal
Not all of them will be the same
True on actual flowers too
Some petals may touch
Some may not
They might overlap
Now time for the details
And to add color!!

What Color is a Blessing?

What color is a blessing?
Blessings can grow
Grass grows, so would green be a good choice?
Blessings can shine and brighten dark places
The sun fills the sky with light, so would yellow be an option?
Blessings can feel like a comforting hug
Just like when I am wrapped up in my comfy blanket, so would purple work?
Blessings can be easy to find if you look for them
Construction cones are easy to see, so would orange be a good choice?
Blessings can hide in unexpected places
Like the night with the stars overhead, so would dark blue be an option?
Blessings can make your heart so happy

www.ingramcontent.com/pod-product-compliance
Lightning Source LLC
Chambersburg PA
CBHW051723130826
49812CB00034B/1313
9789357440622